Beetles

by **Trudi Strain Trueit**

Reading Consultant: Nanci R. Vargus, Ed.D.

Marshall Cavendish
Benchmark
New York

Picture Words

 beetle

 beetles

 branch

 fern

 flower

 girl

 leaf

 rock

 sand

3

 are in many places.

See the on the .

See the on the .

See the on the .

See the 🪲 on the 🌿.

See the on the .

See the on the .

See the on the .

See the on me!

Word to Know

fern (furn)
    a plant with feather-like leaves.

Find Out More

Books

Allman, Tony. *From Jewel Beetles to Fire Sensors*. Detroit, MI: KidHaven Press, 2007.

Lockwood, Sophie. *Beetles*. Mankato, MN: Child's World, 2008.

Sexton, Colleen. *Beetles*. Minneapolis, MN: Bellwether Media, 2007.

DVDs

Insects. TMW Media Group, 2008.

The Jeff Corwin Experience: Insects and Arachnids. Discovery Education, 2005.

Web Sites

ABC-Kid.Com: Beetles
http://www.abc-kid.com/beetles/

National Geographic for Kids: Dung Beetles
http://kids.nationalgeographic.com/Animals/CreatureFeature/Dung-beetle

The San Diego Zoo: Beetle-Mania
http://www.sandiegozoo.org/animalbytes/t-beetle.html

About the Author

Trudi Strain Trueit has written more than forty nonfiction books for children, from early readers to biographies to self-help books for teens. She writes fiction, too, and is the author of the popular *Julep O'Toole* series for middle grade readers. Born and raised in the Pacific Northwest, Trudi lives near Seattle, Washington, with her husband. She has a B.A. in broadcast journalism. She loves photography, art, and gardening. Learn more about Trudi and her books at **www.truditrueit.com**.

About the Reading Consultant

Nanci R. Vargus, Ed.D., used to teach first grade. Now she works at the University of Indianapolis. Nanci helps young people become teachers. She enjoyed seeing all the beetles at the Insect Zoo at the National Museum of Natural History in Washington, D.C.

Marshall Cavendish Benchmark
99 White Plains Road
Tarrytown, NY 10591-5502
www.marshallcavendish.us

All Internet addresses were correct at the time of printing.

Library of Congress Cataloging-In-Publication Data

Trueit, Trudi Strain.
Beetles / by Trudi Strain Trueit.
        p. cm. — (Benchmark rebus. Creepy critters)
Summary: "Easy to read text with rebuses explores beetle varieties"—Provided by publisher.
ISBN 978-0-7614-3962-2
Beetles—Juvenile literature. I. Title.
QL576.2T78 2010
595.76—dc22
        2008023153

Editor: Christine Florie
Publisher: Michelle Bisson
Art Director: Anahid Hamparian
Series Designer: Virginia Pope

Photo research by Connie Gardner

Rebus images provided courtesy of *Dorling Kindersley*.

Cover photo by Digital vision/SuperStock

The photographs in this book are used by permission and through the courtesy of:
Corbis: p. 7 Volkmar Brockhaus; p. 11 Michael and Patricia Fogden; p. 15 Frank Lukasseck; p. 17 Borrell Casais; p. 21 Ausioeser; *Getty Images*: p. 19 Tim Hall; p. 9 Tohoku Images; *Minden Pictures*: p. 13 Michael and Patricia Fogden; *Photo Researchers*: p. 5 Wayne G. Lawler.

Printed in Malaysia
1 3 5 6 4 2